HODDER ENGLISH

The Crucible

In this book you will follow the developing drama of Arthur Miller's play act by act, reading ahead and then working through the tasks and questions. You will develop your skills as:

SPEAKERS AND LISTENERS

by engaging in role play and improvisation
by working with others to discuss and interpret the play
by reading aloud and performing scenes from the play

READERS

by reading the entire play and bringing it to life as a drama
by tracing the development of plot, character and theme
by reading between the lines to discover the implications of the text

WRITERS

by keeping logs to track the development of plot and character
by writing critical essays about the play's key themes
by writing about the characters' thoughts and feelings in the form of diaries

BEFORE YOU START READING ACT ONE

WHISPERS *A WHOLE GROUP ACTIVITY*

- Choose a phrase from the selection below (or make up one of your own if you wish). Try to remember it perfectly. Then, when your teacher tells you, walk around the room whispering your phrase every time you come close to another person. You might want to gradually increase the sound from a whisper to a chant to make the atmosphere more 'spooky'.

'we're on the edge of the wilderness'

'I've seen her dancing naked'

'don't venture out unless you have to'

'she were swaying like a dumb beast'

'I heard a screeching'

'Have you seen the eyes in the forests?'

'the forest is the devil's last preserve'

'our candle will light the world!'

'May the Lord bless us'

'witchcraft they say!'

'abominations are done in the forest'

'these are cruel times'

'the devil's touch is heavier than sick... it's death you know'

'We must perform God's will'

'they say she's a temptress'

After this activity, stop and think about a small village of people miles and miles away from civilisation, on the edge of a wilderness. In the whispering activity, you have heard some of their thoughts and feelings.

What impression do you have of these people and their state of mind?

They existed. They were the people who lived in Salem, a small village in America. They were among the first Europeans to arrive in America. They lived on the frontier, and did not know what lay beyond it. Most of them were farmers and their life was hard. They were serious-minded people who believed in God, the Devil and witchcraft.

The play you are about to read is based on events that happened in this town in 1692. The characters were real people.

RUMOURS *AN ACTIVITY IN THREES*

Decide who shall be **A**, **B** and **C**. Read the box below which corresponds with your letter and study the information in it carefully.

A The forest that surrounds your village on three sides is widely regarded as 'the Devil's land'. You are to make up a story about mysterious goings on in the woods which are linked to the Devil. Try to make the story as believable as possible. Remember the year is 1692, when people were very superstitious. Be prepared to tell this story to other members of your group.

B American Indians live in the land to the west of your village, including parts of the forest and beyond. There is little understanding between the Indian community and yours. You are to make up a story about a meeting, sighting or attack involving Indians nearby. Be prepared to tell this story to other members of your group.

17th Century drawing

C You believe in God and the Devil. Mysterious events have been happening for quite some time now. Some people talk of eyes in the forests, strange rituals and dancing to weird music. What might you have heard? Express some of your feelings, anxieties and suspicions to others in the group.

- Share your stories with each other and discuss them as if you were people in the village.

- Afterwards, consider your thoughts and feelings. Did the rumours frighten or excite you?

Think of examples of rumours you have heard and discussed. Why do rumours start and how are they carried? Can you see any parallels with the rumours in Salem?

FIRST IMPRESSIONS

- Read Miller's description of the stage after the words 'ACT ONE: An overture', then skip a few pages and read the next stage instruction just before the script itself starts.

- Make a rough sketch of the stage from the audience's point of view at the moment Tituba pops her head round the door.

- What first impression might the audience get about the setting and the possible story from this opening view?

- The audience would, of course, know the name of the play. What is a crucible? What does the title suggest?

We are lucky that Arthur Miller, the playwright, has included some notes to accompany the script. In the notes, he explains his thinking about the characters and their motives as well as the underlying causes of their behaviour.

The play is about a witch hunt that really happened. At a time of fear and suspicion, neighbours accused each other of witchcraft: a practice that was punishable by death.

It is interesting and important to know that Arthur Miller wrote the play in 1954, when a modern witch hunt was in progress in America – for anyone suspected of being a communist or a friend of communism.

Discuss what you know and believe about witchcraft.

ACT ONE

Read Act One up to Miller's notes about Putnam. In case any of the words in Act One are unfamiliar to you, there is a vocabulary list on page 11.

'THE RUMOUR OF WITCHCRAFT IS ALL ABOUT'

- Working in pairs:

Step 1

Choose three events that are said to have taken place according to Parris.

Step 2

With your partner (or you could work in a group of three) create three **'still images'** as if those events have been caught on camera. One member of the class could be Parris and kneel in the centre of the room in a praying position: these images are his nightmare.

Step 3

Choose one of the pictures you have created and perform it for the rest of the class. It is best to count down from 3 to 1 and then hold the freeze for about 30 seconds. If space is available, several groups can show their freezes at the same time so that others can see the many fears crowding in on Parris.

- Write a diary entry for Parris at this point in the play, describing his reaction to Betty's condition, expressing his fears about recent events and anxieties about the future.

Still image – sometimes called a 'freeze frame' or 'tableau'. Characters take up position as if the camera caught the act. It can be 'brought to life' if necessary, or the drama can be slowed down to reveal individual characters' thoughts about the scene being depicted.

• What impression have you gained of Abigail so far? What further information would you need to be sure of her honesty? Look carefully at the stage directions (eg 'studies her, then nods, half convinced') and at the dialogue. What does Parris make of Abigail?

Read about Thomas Putnam in Miller's notes, then continue reading the play up to the entry of John Proctor.

Putnam believes there is witchcraft at work. He asks his wife to give the evidence. What is it? It won't convince *you*, but would *he* have believed it?

Try looking at it another way. What would motivate Putnam to stick to his argument even if he didn't quite believe it himself?

The girls reveal the truth about the night in the woods. What are the facts?

Do these facts add up to witchcraft or merely a case of high spirits that has got out of hand?

How do you account for the illnesses?

JOHN PROCTOR

Read Miller's introduction to John Proctor up to Miller's next note about Rebecca Nurse.

What have you decided about past events between John and Abigail?

What fresh insights have you gained into the character of Abigail?

What are your first impressions of John Proctor? Consider:

- what Miller tells us about him in the notes

- his treatment of Mary Warren

- the facts of his past with Abigail

- his mixed feelings about her

- his attitude to the business of witchcraft.

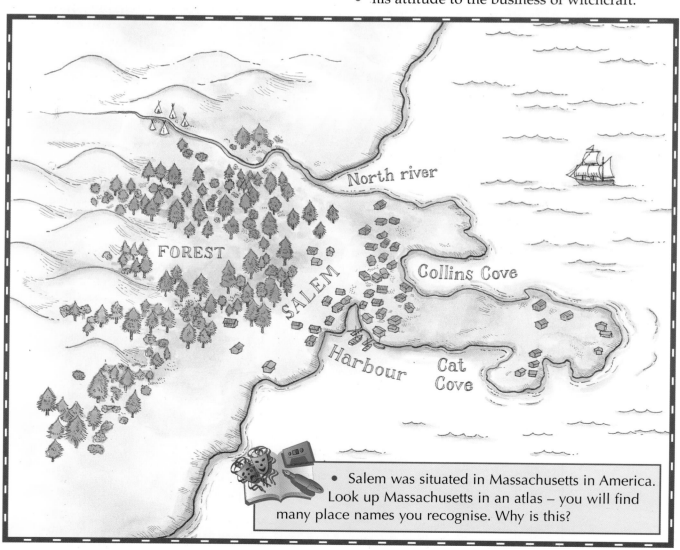

- Salem was situated in Massachusetts in America. Look up Massachusetts in an atlas – you will find many place names you recognise. Why is this?

CRACKS IN THE COMMUNITY

Read on, up to the entrance of Hale, and Miller's next notes.

Parris faces a number of problems as a minister, which are now becoming apparent. Are Parris's demands reasonable?

What is revealed about Putnam in his claim that Proctor took lumber from his land?

Who do you believe and why?

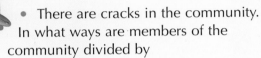

- There are cracks in the community. In what ways are members of the community divided by
   wealth?
   status?
   religion?
   outlook?

In each case, group the characters to show on which side of the crack they stand. Which characters are difficult to place? Why?

IMPROVISATION
IN GROUPS OF SIX

- Take one of the following parts A–F each.

A You have paid for your land over several years and now you want to expand. There is no land left in the town itself, so you hope to cultivate new land outside the town. This will make you more independent, able to make a little money, and live more comfortably.

B You live on the far edge of Salem. You don't care for the strict laws and narrow-mindedness of the leaders there. You keep out of their way as much as possible. You would welcome belonging to a new community of like-minded people.

C You are old, realistic, fair, open-minded and not easily shocked. You are God-fearing, kind and sympathetic. You also have a sense of right and wrong.

D You are a community leader in Salem. You have heard unpleasant rumours that your enemies in the community are on the brink of setting up a separate community. Besides, the land they want to farm is land you had your own eye on. It's not fair: they already own the best land on that side of the town.

E You don't care much for the strict laws in Salem, and you quite like the people who live at the far edge of the community, but you depend on the community leader for your livelihood and you can't risk upsetting him. For the sake of a quiet life, you take his side.

F You represent the church in Salem. You have heard unpleasant rumours that some of your flock are setting up a rival parish on the edge of Salem. Recently, you've noticed that they've virtually stopped coming to church. You take this as a personal insult. To your mind, they are Godless, wicked people who need their come-uppance.

- Hold a meeting.

   – **A** should begin by testing the water: how would the group feel if those living on the far side of Salem – already a small community – set up a small parish next door?

   – Allow people to respond.

   – Develop the argument.

   – Allow the temperature of discussion to rise.

   There is no need to come to an agreement. Allow **C** to close the discussion when it is clear that it can't go any further.

The people of Salem undoubtedly felt strongly about these issues in their community. However, it is unlikely that they would have held a public meeting to express their views. What might they have been afraid of?

Lacking open discussion, how might people vent their feelings on others?

WITCH HUNTING

Read to the end of Act One.

- Put yourself in the position of Reverend Hale. You are on the look-out for the evidence of witchcraft. Read through and make a list of all the evidence you find.

- Imagine you are an ordinary villager. What hopes would you have of Reverend Hale? What fears do you have of Hale? Share your thoughts with a partner.

- Imagine you are Abigail. Read closely her responses to Hale's questions from *'Abigail, what sort of dancing were you doing with her in the forest?'* up to *'She made me drink blood!'* What is Abigail thinking? Make notes on each of her answers to reveal how she is trying to avoid exposure.

- How do you account for Tituba's confessions?

Miller wrote *The Crucible* in response to a period in American history when there was widespread fear of communism. In the 1950s America entered a period of deep mistrust towards Communist Russia. From 1950 until 1954 the USA was swept with anti-communist hysteria. Many Americans believed that they were surrounded by communists who were out to destroy the American way of life. People were persuaded to spy on neighbours, colleagues and friends if they were thought to be communists or communist sympathisers. Millions of names were passed on to the authorities during this period.

(Pages 28–30 provide a more detailed background to the play.)

Communism is a movement based on the common ownership of all property – there is no private property.

Look back again over the last pages of Act One. How do you think Miller is trying to draw a parallel between the events of 1692 and those in the twentieth century? What do you think his view is? Look up any words you find puzzling – 'diabolism', for example.

Senator McCarthy and his Committee on Un-American Activities hold a meeting to inquire into allegations that certain employees of the US delegation to the United Nations were or had been Communists, 1953. (See also pages 28–29)

AFTER READING ACT ONE

KEY MOMENTS

- Choose three scenes from Act One and produce a series of still images to represent each scene.

Some examples might be:

- Reverend Parris praying as Tituba enters/exits

- Abigail, Betty and Mercy alone after the adults leave

- Abigail and Proctor after Mercy leaves them alone together

- the confrontation between Parris and Putnam, Giles and Proctor

- the interrogation of Tituba and her confession

- Abigail's wild accusations.

- For each still image choose an extract from the text and use it as a label for each scene. You may write the label on a large sheet of paper or narrate the extract during the still image.

KEEPING A LOG OF THE PLOT

- Record the key events of the plot on a flow chart down the left-hand side of your page. Start like this:

Parris at Betty's bedside

↓

Parris questions Abigail

↓

The Putnams voice their suspicions

↓

The girls discuss their night in the forest

⋮

Now continue from the entry of John Proctor.

- Use the right hand column to record anything you find particularly significant about the scene. For example:

The girls discuss their night in the forest.	*Facts at last. Abigail the ringleader.*

- Fill in the log up to the end of Act One.

KEEPING A CHARACTER LOG

- Reserve one sheet of paper for each character.

- Draw a figure at the top of the page and surround it with the factual information you have gathered about that character from Miller's descriptions and from the text. Look at the example on the opposite page.

- Divide the rest of the page into three columns. In the left-hand column note down aspects of their character as they emerge. In the middle column record a quote or example as evidence of this character trait. In the right-hand column record the page number.

- On the reverse side, keep a note of their appearances in each Act, what they do and any significant contribution they make to events.

For example, John Proctor in Act One:

At Parris's house

- sends Mary Warren home

- rejects Abigail's advances

- dismisses the talk of witchcraft

- heated discussion with Parris about the church

- heated discussion with Putnam about land rights

CHARACTER LOG

John Proctor

Powerfully built

Doesn't suffer fools

Steady

Decent

Farmer

Mid-30s

A sharp manner

'A sinner'

Aspects of his character	Evidence	Page
Quick tempered	Shaking Abby: 'Do you look for a whippin'?'	

ROLE IN PLOT

Act 1

Act 2

Act 3

Act 4

Act 5

HELP

VOCABULARY

There are a number of words in Act One that may seem unfamiliar. Here is a guide to some of these words.

'hearty' – healthy

'dissembling' – lying or misleading

'heathen' – anyone not Christian (e.g. American Indians)

'trafficked' – communicated

'abominations' – evil things

'Goody [Proctor]' – wife of or Mrs

'clamoured intentions' – disturbed by suspicions

'a pointy reckoning' – revenge with a knife or dagger

'covenanted' – Christians by oath

'Quakers' – members of a religious society who believed in peaceful principles and plainness of dress

'break charity' – break friends

'spoke Barbados' – in the language of Barbados (people from Salem would not have understood it)

Clare Holman as Abigail and Tom Wilkinson as John Proctor, National Theatre, 1990

ACT TWO

A vocabulary list for this act is provided on page 15.

ELIZABETH AND JOHN PROCTOR

Look carefully at the scene between Elizabeth and Proctor up to the entrance of Mary Warren. This scene is tense because John and Elizabeth do not really say what they are thinking. The tension rises until John finally relents.

READING BETWEEN THE LINES

- Act out this scene in groups of four. Two people need to play the part of Elizabeth. One represents her inner thoughts, one her spoken ones. The same applies to John Proctor.

Character	Real speech	Thoughts
Elizabeth	'What keeps you so late? It's almost dark'	'I wonder where you really were?'
John	'I were out planting far out to the forest edge'	'Is she thinking of Abigail I wonder?'

Inner-outer thoughts – the means by which a conflict between what a character thinks and what he/she says can be revealed.

A DEVELOPING CRISIS

Read on up to the exit of Mary Warren.
What is happening in Salem?
Why has the witch hunt taken hold?
Consider Mary Warren's position. What is
motivating her?

> • Write your own newspaper
> headline and two or three short
> paragraphs that might have been published in
> the Salem paper the next day.

SALEM HERALD
39 IN COMPACT WITH LUCIFER!

**Salem people have been shocked to
discover that, following confessions
made by a Miss Abigail Williams,
over thirty women have been
arrested on suspicion of dabbling
with the devil.**

**It began eight days ago when
Miss Betty Parris fell into a state
of nervous convulsion accompanied
by screaming.**

Since then . . .

ELIZABETH CONFRONTS JOHN

Read on from the exit of Mary Warren up to the entrance of Hale.

Act out this scene between Elizabeth
and John.

- Choose one person to play the part of John,
  and another to play the part of Elizabeth.

- The whole group should sit around an acting
  space in two semi-circles forming a main
  circle.

- Decide on the actual space, any props, and
  then 'direct' the two actors. Discuss how they

might play their parts, paying particular
attention to:

– tone of voice

– gesture

– use of pause.

- Run through the scene a few times, stopping
  when necessary to offer advice before re-
  running the scene. When the group feels
  satisfied with the performance, stop.

Defining space – the process by which a
group decide on the boundaries in which the
drama is set. For example: 'Let us imagine
the village ends here… beyond this line is
no-man's land.

Consider carefully whether Elizabeth is correct
when she tells John Proctor that Abigail 'has an
arrow in you yet'.

Is John right when he says 'I have forgot
Abigail'?

WHO IS TELLING THE TRUTH?

- Place Elizabeth (a volunteer to play the part) in the centre of the room. Stand in relation to how close you feel she is to the truth. Stand near her if you think she is right to challenge John about Abigail. Stand some distance away from her if you are not sure. Finally, if you disagree, stand at the edge of the room. This will give you an idea of how everyone feels on this issue.

- As a group, select a few people from each position and ask them to adopt a role as a citizen of Salem. Perhaps they could say what they're thinking about Elizabeth or John Proctor, for example: 'They're a hard-working couple. I trust them.' or 'He always struck me as someone with something to hide… she's no better.'

INTERROGATION

Read on up to the entry of Giles Corey. The people in this scene choose their words carefully. The following phrases are all designed to disguise something or hint at wider implications.

Hale: 'I have some further travelling yet tonight'

Hale: 'There is a softness in your record, sir, a softness'

Proctor: 'I think it be a small fault'

Proctor: 'Sportin' in the woods'

Proctor: 'Elizabeth, you bewilder him!'

What is the meaning behind each phrase and why are the speakers choosing their words so carefully?

Zoe Wanamaker as Elizabeth, National Theatre, 1990

ACCUSED

Read up to the end of Act Two. Look closely at the accusations made against Martha Corey and Elizabeth Proctor. In the witch hunt, a number of people accuse others for private and malicious reasons. How many such cases can you identify in the play so far?

- Imagine you are called upon to defend Martha Corey and Elizabeth Proctor. Write a short statement claiming their innocence and arguing why you think the evidence against them is false.

Proctor holds back from telling the truth in order to preserve his good name in the community. In contrast, Elizabeth is not afraid to speak the truth. The arrival of Giles near the end of Act Two brings news of his wife's arrest and confirmation of the accusations against Elizabeth. You have now met all of the main characters in the play except for Danforth.

- How does each character react to the news of the latest accusations? Copy and complete the chart below to help you.

Character	Quote
John Proctor	'There are them that will swear to anything'
Elizabeth Proctor	
Mary Warren	
Reverend Hale	
Francis Nurse	
Giles Corey	
Ezekiel Cheever	

- Choose one of the major characters from the list above and write two diary entries to cover Act One and Act Two. Include what you believe to be the thoughts and feelings of your chosen character, as well as the main events from his or her point of view.

- Update your plot and character charts.

HELP

VOCABULARY

'Lucifer' – another name for the Devil

'Devil's bitch' – an evil spirit

'I'd as lief' – I would rather

'Pontius Pilate' – a Roman official who chose not to judge Christ but let a local mob decide his fate, thus washing his hands of the responsibility for judgement

'lechery' – lust, adultery

BEFORE READING ACT THREE

Look at the illustration showing six demonic incidents, from Glanvill's book *Saducismus Triumphatus*. They give us a good idea of the kinds of activities in which accused witches were said to take part.

• Make up a story that might be told to a neighbour involving one of these scenes and tell it to another person in the group. See if they can guess to which incident your story relates.

WITCH HUNTS

A witch hunt is defined as 'a rigorous campaign to round up or expose dissenters on the pretext of safeguarding the public welfare' *(Collins English Dictionary)*.

The belief in witchcraft was common throughout medieval Europe and convicted witches (mainly women) were often burnt at the stake, drowned, beheaded or tortured before they confessed (often to crimes they could not possibly have committed). In England 'witches' were treated less harshly as a rule but the belief that they existed and brought harm to communities was widely held throughout the middle ages. This belief in witchcraft created a visible enemy of Christianity. People believed that the Devil was engaged in a constant battle for Christian souls.

The puritans who discovered New England shared the beliefs common in England at the time. Their fear of the unknown world to the west of their village only made them more vulnerable to the threat and myth of witchcraft. The people of Salem (and Andover, a village nearby) lived a hard life on the fringes of a huge continent still peopled by American Indians who were resentful of the invasion of the white people. They felt under seige and so they stuck together. The strict Protestant religion held political as well as religious power.

Another factor which promoted the belief in witchcraft was that it was profitable. The property and belongings of the 'witch' could be seized after execution.

The Witches of Mora, Sweden, being burnt. Engraving 1670

Witches Sabbath by Frans Francken, early 17th Century

HYSTERIA

There has been much debate about the nature of the girls' illnesses. Why did they make accusations of witchcraft and act in a way that made people believe they were 'possessed by the Devil'? Tituba probably told the girls stories about fortune-telling and witchcraft, which made an impression on them. They would have found these stories fascinating but then experienced guilt feelings arising from their enjoyment of such 'forbidden information'. They probably suffered from what modern scholars call 'mass-hysteria', not unlike the kind of hysteria we see at rock concerts or celebrity receptions.

ACT THREE

Act Three opens one week later and is set in the ante-room of the General Court in Salem. Notice that all these settings in the text seem claustrophobic and gloomy. Why is this, do you think?

A vocabulary list for this Act is provided on page 20.

Read up to Parris: 'He's come to overthrow this court, your honour' – about seven pages of text.

PLEADING

In this section Giles and Francis have come to the General Court to try to make the judge see reason. They have a strong case. Why are they not successful?

In retrospect, what advice would you have given them about presenting their case?

What are your first impressions of Danforth?

When you have considered these questions, complete the task on the right.

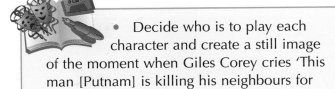

- Decide who is to play each character and create a still image of the moment when Giles Corey cries 'This man [Putnam] is killing his neighbours for their land!'

- Decide which characters would:
  - agree with Giles' statement
  - disagree with Giles' statement
  - find it difficult to give an honest answer.

- Now each person in the image should speak their mind.

- Discuss what this reveals about the trial.

A CHANCE TO PUT THINGS RIGHT

Read on up to the entrance of the girls to be questioned.

John Proctor comes quite close here to setting the record straight. Use the information in the text to work out what he has been doing between Act Two and Act Three.

Why does Hale urge Danforth to wait until a lawyer can handle the matter for Proctor?

THE CLIMAX

Read on from the entrance of the girls to the end of the scene.

- In small groups, act out the whole scene. Each character will need to write notes next to their lines to help guide them. An example is given below:

```
┌─────── aloud ───────┐    ┌─── lower voice – to Danforth only: urgent, ───┐
                                        sincere, desperate.
```

– **Hale:** *Excellency, it is a natural lie to tell; I beg you, stop now before another is condemned.*

- Consider the ways in which you could create a tense atmosphere. Re-run the scene as a group until you find the means of establishing and maintaining tension. Consider the use of pause, gesture, eye contact and intonation in the voice. Bear in mind that the results of this trial are far-reaching.

Mary Warren and John Proctor have decided to reveal the truth because they believe it is important despite the cost to themselves.

Ironically, Elizabeth Proctor's decision to lie because of her deep love for John Proctor ultimately condemns him as a liar.

Notice also how Abigail's powerful performance reduces Danforth to near hysteria.

Royal Exchange Theatre, Manchester, 1990

- What questions would you ask Hale, Danforth, Mary Warren and others? Get into a small group and work out some questions you would like to ask them if you could.

- Now arrange your chairs into a broad semi-circle or horseshoe shape. Put a chair in a position facing the horseshoe. Ask for volunteers to play the parts of Mary Warren, Danforth, Hale (plus others of your choice). Ask them questions (they must answer in the role of the character) relating to the trial scene. This process is called 'hot-seating'.

- Update your plot and character logs, taking into account the events of Act Three.

Hot-seating involves interviewing characters in role to find out their thinking and/or motives for doing what they did.

HELP

VOCABULARY

'broke charity' – betrayed

'affidavit' – a written statement produced for the court

'deposition' – testimony on oath

'Cain and Abel' – In the bible Cain killed his brother Abel – it was supposedly the first murder in the world

'ipso facto' – Latin for: by that very fact

'probity' – honesty

'perjury' – lying to the court

'rung the doom' – announced the fate, ruin of

ACT FOUR

Before you start to read Act Four, consider the possible endings to the play. Which do you think is most likely?

THE SETS

- Draw the set for Act Four using Miller's directions. What impact would this set have on the audience as Act Four commences?

- Look back over the sets for each Act. Do you notice any pattern or theme in them?

IN SALEM JAIL

Read up to Danforth's cry 'Mr Parris, you are a brainless man!' A vocabulary list for this Act is provided on page 23.

How have things changed? Consider characters, events and attitudes.

- In pairs, improvise and re-enact the scene in which Abigail and Mercy leave Salem by stealth. Take into account the fact that Parris's strongbox has been opened.

REBELLION

Read on to Parris's 'Hush' as Elizabeth Proctor enters. What is the nature of the 'rebellion'? What form does it take? How likely is it to succeed?

Look at Hale's comment below:

Excellency, there are orphans wandering from house to house; abandoned cattle on the highroads, the stink of rotting crops hangs everywhere, and no man knows when the harlot's cry will end his life – and you wonder yet if rebellion's spoke. Better you should marvel how they do not burn your province.

WRITING HISTORY *AN EXERCISE FOR TWO GROUPS*

- Imagine you are writing an entry in a history book which records the scenes in Salem in the weeks following the trial:

  Group A can write freely and can describe the situation as it really is. There are no restrictions. Try to show how those in authority made important mistakes in the 'witch hunt'.

  Group B face restrictions. Imagine that this history book is subject to censorship by the authorities in Salem. You cannot be openly critical and yet you have to reflect events as people might have seen them.

- Display these entries on the wall and/or ensure that group A and B swap papers.

Censorship is the process by which all or part of any newspaper article, book, play, letter and so on is suppressed, often on the grounds that it is not 'in the public interest'.

'THAT BE THE DEVIL'S ARGUMENT'

Read on to Parris 'God lead you now,' just before Elizabeth is left alone with Proctor.

The scene between Hale and Elizabeth is important. Do you agree with Hale?

Why does Elizabeth respond in this way?

DECISIONS

Read on to the re-entry of Danforth.

Elizabeth gives Proctor the news of those who have confessed or died, and she tells him of Giles Corey's death. Read the account carefully.

- In small groups show a still image of Giles Corey's torture just before death.

- Consider John's reasons for giving in to the pressure to confess. In your own words, express the dilemma he faces.

- Read aloud that part of the scene in which he discusses his decision to confess. Read slowly, leaving pauses between sentences, and in these spaces, consider what feelings both John and Elizabeth experience. The acute sadness of this scene lies in what remains unspoken.

CONCLUSION

Now read to the end of the play.

- First, discuss your reactions to the ending. In what sense is it a satisfying ending?

- In pairs, discuss the following question: How does Rebecca Nurse's refusal to confess affect John Proctor's decision not to do so?

- Why does he rip up his initial confession?

- Does John die without his 'name' or with a good conscience? Explain.

- Compare the ending of the play with the beginning. What are the similarities? What are the differences?

- Update your character and plot logs.

- What is the significance of the last set of stage directions by Miller?

HELP

VOCABULARY

'Majesty' – meaning the devil

'providence' – a blessing

AFTER COMPLETING THE PLAY

AN HISTORICAL PERSPECTIVE

Look carefully at the two transcripts relating to the trial of Bridget Bishop and William Barker respectively. These are original manuscripts from the real Salem witch hunts.

(Bridget Bishop was the first defendant to be tried in court in June 1692).

Transcript of Bishop death warrant and return

To George Corwin Gent^m. High Sheriff of the County of Essex Greeting

Whereas Bridgett Bishop als Olliver the wife of Edward Bishop of Salem in the County of Essex Sawyer at a speciall Court of Oyer and Terminer held at Salem the second Day of this instant month of June for the Counties of Essex Middlesex and Suffolk before William Stoughton Esqr. and his Associate Justices of the said Court was Indicted and arraigned upon five several Indictments for using practising and exercising on the Nineteenth day of April last past and divers other days and time before and after certain acts of Witchcraft in and upon the bodies of Abigail Williams, Ann puttnam Junr., Mercy Lewis, Mary walcott, and Elizabeth Hubbard of Salem village Singlewomen, whereby their boydes were hurt, afflicted, pined, consumed, Wasted and tormented contrary to the form of the statute in that Case made and provided to which Indictm^{ts}. the said Bridgett Bishop pleaded not guilty and for Tryall thereof put herselfe upon God and her Country, whereupon she was found guilty of the felonyes and Witchcrafts whereof she stood Indicted and sentence of Death accordingly passed ag^t. her as the Law directs. Execution whereof yet remains to be done These are therefore in the name of their Majties William and Mary now King & Queen over England &c. to will and Comand you that upon Fryday next being the Tenth day of this instant month of June between the hours of eight and twelve in the aforenoon of the same day You safely conduct the s^d. Bridgett Bishop als Olliver from their Maj.^{ties} gaol in Salem afores^d. to the place of Execution and there cause her to be hanged by the neck untill she be dead and of your doings herein make return to the Clerk of the s^d. Court and p^{r}cept And hereof you are not to fail at your peril. And this shall be your sufficient Warrant Given under my hand & Seal at Boston the Eighth day of June in the fourth year of the Reigne of our Soverign Lord and Lady William & Mary now King & Queen over England &c.

Anno Dom. 1692

Wm Stoughton

June 10th 1692

According to the within written precept I have taken the body of the within named Brigett Bishop out of their Majesties' gaole in Salem and safely conveyed her to the place provided for her Execution and caused y^e sd Brigett to be hanged by the next untill she was dead all which was according to the time within Required and so I make Return by me_____ George Corwin Sheriff

Exhibit 6

Transcript of Barker confession

William Barker of Andovers examination & confession

29. Augst. 92.

Coram

Maj: Gidney

Mr. Hathorn

Mr. Corwin

Cap: Higginson

He confesses he has been in the snare of the devil three years, that the devil first appeared to his lyke a black man and perceived he had a cloven foot, That the devil demanded of him to give up himself soul & Body unto him, which he promised to do. He said he had a great family, the world went hard with him and was willing to pay every man his own, And the devil told him he would pay all his debts and he should live comfortably _____ He confesses he has afflicted Sprague foster and martin, his three accusers That he did signe the devils book with blood brought to him in a thing lyke an Inkhorn that he dipt his finger therein and made a blott in the book which was a confirmation of the Covenant with the devil.

He confesses he was at a meeting of witches at Salem Village where he judges there was about a hundred of them, that the meeting was upon a green piece of ground near the ministers house. He said they mett there to destroy that place by reason of the peoples being divided & there differing with their ministers Satan's design was to set up his own worship, abolish all the churches in the land, to fall next upon Salem and so go through the country He sayth the devil promised that all his people should live bravely that all persons should be equall; that there should be no day of resurrection or of judgement, and neither punishment nor shame for sin _____ He sayth there was a Sacrament at that meeting, there was also bread & wyne Mr Burroughs was a ringleader in that meeting, It was proposed at the meeting to make as many witches as they could, And they were all by Mr. Burroughs and the black man exhorted to pull down the Kingdom of christ and set up the kingdome of the devil. He said he knew Mr Burroughs and Goody How to be such persons, And that he heard a trumpet sounded at the meeting and thinks it was Burroughs that did it. the sound is heard many myles off and then they all come one after another _____ In the spring of the year the witches came from Connecticut to afflict at Salem Village but now they have left it off And that he has been informed by some of the grandees that there is about 307 witches in the country _____ He sayth the witches are much disturbed with the afflicted persons because they are discovered by them, They curse the judges Because their Society is brought under. They would have the afflicted persons counted as witches But he thinks the afflicted persons are Innocent & that they do god good service And that he has not known or heard of one Innocent person taken up & put in prison _____ He saith he is heartily sorry for what he has done and for hurting the afflicted persons his accusers, prayes their forgiveness, desires prayers for himself, promises to renounce the devil and all his works, And then he could take them all by the hand without any harme by his eye or any otherwise _____ the aboveSaid is the Truth as witness my hand:

William Barker

- Choose one transcript to present in a dramatic format. You may choose to re-enact the scene to which William Barker confessed or the acts of which Bridget Bishop was accused.

- Another possibility is to re-enact the trial scene while other members of the group present still images illustrating the acts in which the two were accused of taking part.

- Now write your own scene (including stage directions) based on the time when Abigail Williams was employed by the Proctors. Try to reveal something of each character and the tensions that emerge later.

THE INDIVIDUAL AND SOCIETY

The Crucible is a play about the tensions that exist between the individual and society.

From your point of view

First, think about this issue from your own point of view. There is you as an individual with your own needs and interests, and there is society which is all the people around you organised in the form of family, school, police, council, and so on.

At times you need, depend on and enjoy society – think of some examples.

At other times you are held back, punished and controlled by society – think of some examples.

In Salem

Now think about this issue in seventeenth century Salem. Society in Salem is represented by the villagers, the Church and by the law in the form of Governor Danforth.

In what way does society support the individuals in Salem? Why are they so dependent on it?

In what ways are they held back, punished and controlled by society?

Take Giles Corey as an example:

From society he gets:

Company, love and respect from his family and friends.

A living, because others buy the things he grows on his farm.

The comfort of religion and sharing deeply-held beliefs with others.

The protection of the law when, in the past, he had grievances.

Strength of numbers against the dangers which lie beyond the forest edge.

But he suffers at the hands of society because:

He has to live within the Church's strict rules and expectations.

Rich people like the Putnams tend to get their way, especially in land rights.

The law is most powerful even when it is wrong.

Society is considered more important than the individual in these hard times.

> • Take one major character and one minor character in the play and make a similar list for each of them.

THE ROLE OF WOMEN IN THE PLAY

- **Prepare an essay on the role of women in the play in this way:**

1 List all the women in the play and refresh your memory about them from your character logs.

2 Consider the social position of women in Salem by thinking about the following points:

- what was expected of wives

- what the working women did

- society's view of children

- why they might have felt frustrated

3 The girls in the village

The events in the play are started off by the wild dancing in the forest. Remind yourself what had been going on, and also think about why the girls would have been involved in it. What was the attraction in it?

Later, they allow themselves to be whipped up into hysteria. Give some examples of this and why it might have happened.

During the trials, they accuse others of witchcraft. Why do they do this if it isn't true? Describe the pressures they were under.

4 Abigail

Abigail is an unusual character in the play, because she knows how to exploit people and how to look after herself. She is intelligent and quick-witted, but selfish.

Before looking at her guilty role in the play, can you find anything to admire in her, or identify ways in which she herself has been hurt by society?

Now think about her role in the witch hunt. Why does she do it? Look at those moments when she stirs up the situation, such as the very last page of Act One or the moment she spots the yellow bird in court. What prompts her?

5 The wives

What fine qualities do they have?

Why do the wives make easy victims?

Describe the dilemmas faced by Elizabeth Proctor: before the play opens (knowing her husband had an affair with Abigail); during the play (knowing that Abigail is lying); and at the end of the play (wanting her husband to live but unwilling to give in to lies).

6 Just deserts

Consider each group of women. Who gets their just deserts? Who, at the end of the play, do you admire, despise and blame?

Young Vic, 1985

BACKGROUND: MILLER AND THE AMERICA OF THE 1950S

Arthur Miller said of his play, 'I believe that the reader will discover here the essential nature of one of the strangest and most awful events in history'.

Senator Joe McCarthy was the leading figure of the anti-communist movement. He chaired the Committee on Un-American Activities which attempted to purge America of communism. This committee had the power to put people 'on trial'. Those accused had to answer questions about their habits, friends, political beliefs, and name other people whom they might suspect of being communists. If these people refused to appear they might find themselves 'blacklisted', which meant that they would have problems finding or keeping their jobs. Having friends who were communists might mean that you too would be labelled a communist.

Nearly 7000 people working in the civil service between May 1953 and October 1954 lost their jobs because they were considered by the Committee to be security risks. Over three million names were passed on to the Committee, an indication of the fear and extreme mistrust that gripped America in this period.

Writers, actors and people connected with the Hollywood film industry were frequently called before the Committee. Charlie Chaplin was one such victim and he never worked in America again.

The cartoons below show how some commentators judged McCarthy's methods and ideas.

'Here in Washington D.C. from Hollywood, to fight what they call the "Political Inquisition" of the Un-American Activities Committee probe of Communist influences on films, actors and actresses listen attentively. Left to right, 2nd row: *Danny Kaye; Evelyn Keyes; June Havoc; Humphrey Bogart and his wife, Lauren Bacall.* 3rd row: *Joe Sistrom (behind Evelyn Keyes); Ralph Alswang; Sam Wannamaker; Robert Andry, and Richard Conte.' December, 1947*

Read Danforth's statement:

But you must understand, sir, that a person is either with this court or he must be counted against it, there be no road between. This is a sharp time, now, a precise time – we live no longer in the dusky afternoon when evil mixed itself with good and befuddled the world. Now, by God's grace, the shining sun is up, and them that fear not light will surely praise it. I hope you will be one of those.

Compare Danforth's statement with this comment by Arthur Miller about the American 'witch hunt' for communists:

In America any man who is not a reactionary [right wing] in his views is open to the charge of alliance with Red hell [communism]. Political opposition, thereby, is given an inhuman overlay which then justifies the abrogation [cancellation] of all normally applied customs of civilized intercourse. A political policy is equated with moral right, and opposition to it with diabolical malevolence [evil].

McCarthy's witch hunt led to investigation into the lives of more than nine million people. Very few people dared to oppose Senator McCarthy.

What links are there between McCarthyism and the witch hunts in Salem?

Look at the following statements about the McCarthy witch hunts. Copy and complete the table to show how they have a parallel with events in Salem. Add to it if you can.

McCarthy witch hunts	Salem
Mass hysteria spread among people who feared a communist takeover	*Hysteria breaks out as people believe witchcraft is evident*
Power was in the hands of the judges	
People were asked to name neighbours, friends and acquaintances who might be communists	
Any man or woman who was not reactionary (right wing) could be charged with forming an allegiance with the Red hell (communism)	
a climate of fear became established	
McCarthy was ruthless in his search for 'reds under the bed'	

CHARACTERISATION

Look at the list of those who died in the witch hysteria of 1692.

A List of Those Persons Who Died During The Witch Hysteria of 1692

SARAH OSBORNE
of Salem Village died in jail May 10.
BRIDGET BISHOP
of Salem Village, hanged June 10.
UNNAMED CHILD
under one year, belonging to Sarah Good died in jail previous to July 19.
SARAH GOOD
of Salem Village, hanged July 19.
ELIZABETH HOW
of Topsfield, hanged July 19.
SUSANNAH MARTIN
Of Amesbury, hanged July 19.
REBECCA NURSE
of Salem Village, hanged July 19.
SARAH WILDES
of Topsfield, hanged July 19.
REVEREND GEORGE BURROUGHS
of Wells, Maine, formerly minister at Salem Village, hanged August 19.
MARTHA CARRIER
of Andover, hanged August 19.
GEORGE JACOBS
of Salem, hanged August 19.
JOHN PROCTOR
of Salem Village, hanged August 19.

JOHN WILLARD
of Salem Village, hanged August 19.
ANN FOSTER
of Andover died in jail as a confessed witch sometime after September 10.
GILES COREY
of Salem Village, pressed to death September 19.
MARTHA COREY
of Salem Village, hanged September 22.
MARY ESTY
of Topsfield, hanged September 22.
ALICE PARKER
of Salem, hanged September 22.
MARY PARKER
of Andover, hanged September 22
ANN PUDEATOR
of Salem, hanged September 22.
WILMOT REED
of Marblehead, hanged September 22.
MARGARET SCOTT
of Rowley, hanged September 22.
SAMUEL WARDWELL
of Andover, hanged September 22.
SARAH DASTIN
of Reading, pardoned during the 'jail delivery' in May 1693. She died in jail unable to pay her jail fees.

- Write a suitable **epitaph** for four characters from the list using evidence from the text. The epitaph should be 50 words excluding biographical detail.

- Choose one figure from the play and explain his or her character, role and development in the play.

  – Provide factual information about the character.

  – Comment on their introduction into the play.

  – Follow their personal development and their impact on the plot act by act.

  – Summarise the significance of the character.

  Avoid retelling the story, but do consult your character logs to help you with this exercise.

An **epitaph** is the inscription on a gravestone, or a funeral address describing the qualities of someone who has died.

EXTENSION TASKS

The following tasks will give you opportunities to revise and develop what you have learned in this book.

- Discuss the role of two or more minor characters in the play.
  For this essay, you might choose to consider:

  The girls

  Tituba (explaining her position in Salem and what we know of her character, and her important role in the opening crisis)

  Herrick (as a petty official who is given a sense of power by the trial)

  The wives other than Elizabeth (explaining how they are victims of the witch hunt but also contribute to it)

- What is the moral of the story?
  This is an essay about the themes and messages of the play. You could consider:

  The importance of keeping faith with yourself and your loved ones.

  The dangers of being too blinkered, fearful and uncompromising, and how this relates to the Church in Salem.

  What happens when people lack democracy, free speech and freedom of choice.

  The parallels with anti-communism and other modern witch hunts, moral panics and scare stories.

  Whether the fate of the characters is a just one.

- Take one scene and demonstrate Miller's skill as a playwright.

  Choose a key scene such as the yellow bird scene, the last scene between Elizabeth and Proctor, or any other you found especially interesting. A good way to prepare for this

essay is to take act it out, taking the role of director of a small group who act out the chosen scene.
You should produce:

- An annotated copy of the script with your ideas for the characters, movements, and delivery.

- Notes to each key actor about how you want the scene to be played and delivered.

- A short essay pointing out the elements which make good drama in this scene. You could comment on:

  How mood, tension and suspense are built up.

  How the words, actions and even the pauses play on the emotions.

  The language of the characters.

  Timing, pace.

  Moments of particular impact and what makes them so significant.

  The significance of the scene to the play as a whole.

You should cover all these points, but as they may overlap, do plan how you are going to sequence them. It may be easiest to work through the scene, commenting on all of them as you go, but stopping to discuss significant points in more depth.

- What challenges would designers face in producing this play?

  How would they be resolved?

  Consider the demands of:
  – sets
  – costumes
  – make-up
  – lighting